199 ideas

Raising Revenue

PUBLISHED BY

ASAE: THE CENTER FOR ASSOCIATION LEADERSHIP

The Center for Association Leadership

WASHINGTON, DC

The contributors have worked diligently to ensure that all information in this book is accurate as of the time of publication and consistent with standards of good practice in the general management community. As research and practice advance, however, standards may change. For this reason it is recommended that readers evaluate the applicability of any recommendations in light of particular situations and changing standards.

ASAE: The Center for Association Leadership
1575 I Street, NW
Washington, DC 20005-1103
Phone: (202) 626-2723; (888) 950-2723 outside the metropolitan Washington, DC
   area
Fax: (202) 220-6439
Email: books@asaecenter.org
We connect great ideas and great people to inspire leadership and achievement in the association community.

Keith C. Skillman, CAE, Vice President, Publications, ASAE: The Center for
   Association Leadership
Baron Williams, CAE, Director of Book Publishing, ASAE: The Center for Association
   Leadership

Cover design by Beth Lower, Art Director, ASAE: The Center for Association
   Leadership and Troy Scott Parker, Cimarron Design
Interior design by Troy Scott Parker, Cimarron Design

This book is available at a special discount when ordered in bulk quantities. For information, contact the ASAE Member Service Center at (202) 371-0940.

A complete catalog of titles is available on the ASAE: The Center for Association Leadership website at www.asaecenter.org/bookstore.

ISBN-13: 978-0-88034-330-5
ISBN-10: 0-88034-330-3

Printed in the United States of America.

10 9 8 7 6 5 4 3 2

CONTENTS

INTRODUCTION AND ACKNOWLEDGMENTS

Raising revenue is not only about selling products and services, collecting more dues, or landing more donations and corporate dollars. It's also about developing the right products and services, pricing them appropriately, building and maintaining relationships with the people and corporations who give you money, and paying attention to the underlying structure and culture that support revenue raising. Equally important as building revenue streams is finding savings and cost-efficiencies, making the most of what you have, and protecting it by managing your risk. Even 199 ideas about how to achieve these goals constitute a drop in the bucket of possibilities. Undoubtedly, whole books could be filled with idea-starters for fundraising, membership (see *199 Ideas: Membership Recruitment and Retention*, 2009 ASAE and The Center for Association Leadership), sponsorship, and any other topic discussed in this publication.

Not all of these ideas will apply to your organization. There is no one-size-fits-all money making—or saving—solution for membership organizations, let alone for the entire range of nonprofits. We hope, however, that each of the tips in this book will drive home a fundamental, freshen up an old standard, or spark your imagination in ways that help your organization increase its bottom line.

The ideas here were culled, adapted, and compiled from many years of stories told in ASAE publications and from tips generously contributed by colleagues like you. If you find something here that you can use, please consider giving back to the community by sharing a tip for possible inclusion in future publications. Check out the back pages of this book or go to **www.asaecenter.org/sharemytip**.

Our "199 Ideas" series is always growing, and we're always looking for ideas in many topic areas.

Our sincerest thanks to the following contributors and to all those who share their experiences through ASAE: The Center for Association Leadership:

Aime M. Ballard-Wood (contributor and editor)
Ballard-Wood, LLC
Falls Church, VA

Francie Davenport
Associate Director, Print Production & Merchandizing
American Diabetes Association
Alexandria, VA

William Davis
Web Content Manager
American Society of Consultant Pharmacists
Alexandria, VA

Valerie Jane Fries
Chief of Education
International Right of Way Association
Gardena, CA

Jennifer Proctor
Director, Industry Content
APICS The Association for Operations Management
Chicago, IL

Ann Ranson
Executive Coach, Speaker, Marketer
Dallas, TX

Tanya Tolpegin, CAE
Chief Executive Officer
Society of Cardiovascular Computed Tomography
Vienna, VA

A special thanks to **Aime Ballard-Wood** for not only contributing ideas, but also for serving as editor for this publication.

MEMBERSHIP

Get New Members

1. Make recruiting new members a priority.

You cannot retain your way to growth. No matter how effective your retention program is—and it is vitally important—members will still leave your association, so building a thriving membership acquisition program is fundamental. Survey results in the 2010 Membership Marketing Benchmarking Report indicate that associations that put a higher priority on acquisition than retention are more likely to be increasing their membership numbers.

2. Do not reinvent the membership marketing wheel.

Every organization has unique challenges, but that does not mean that time-tested membership marketing strategies and tactics do not apply. Take time to understand and use the most effective practices that have grown membership for hundreds of associations over the years.

3. Give membership marketing adequate funding.

A member generates a predictable dues income stream over time for an association: For example, an association that charges $200 a year in dues and maintains an 85 percent renewal rate will hold onto a member for an average of 6.66 years and receive $1,332 in lifetime

Using Lifetime Value of Membership

Lifetime Value Measurements	How to Calculate
Lifetime Dues Value of a Member	Yearly dues per member times average member tenure
Annual Nondues Revenue per Member	Total nondues revenue divided by number of members
Lifetime Nondues Value of a Member	Annual nondues revenue divided by number of members times average member tenure
Gross Lifetime Value of a Member	Lifetime dues value plus lifetime nondues value
Lifetime Cost to Serve Member	Annual cost of serving members times average member tenure
Net Lifetime Value of a Member	Gross lifetime value of a member minus lifetime cost to serve member

Example of a Lifetime Value Calculation

Number of Members	12,000
Annual expenses	600,000
Average dues level	$230
Annual nondues revenue	$2,000,000
Average member tenure	7.5 years
Lifetime dues value	$1,725
Annual nondues revenue per member	$167
Lifetime nondues value	$1,250
Gross Life time value	$2,975
Annual cost to serve a member	$50
Lifetime cost to serve a member	$375
Net lifetime value of a member	$2,600

What Does the Lifetime Value Calculation Help You Do?

It helps you determine how much you can spend to acquire new members because it allows you to see where your break-even point is. It is a fair measure of what a members' financial contribution is because it takes into consideration the nondues revenue that a member contributes to the organization.

continued on next page

continued from previous page

What Should Your LTV Look Like?

Typically, LTV will be 7 to 10 times your annual dues amount. It is dependent on the relationship between the dues amount and the amount members contribute via participation in events, purchase of products and services, and other ways members are involved in creating association revenue.

How often should you examine LTV?

Review LTV at least annually, but more often if you are introducing new products and services or if you're seeing major changes in renewal trends.

Reprinted from "Financial Metrics for the Membership Professional," by Susanne Connors Bowman and Lori Gusdorf, CAE, from *Membership Essentials: Recruitment, Retention, Roles, Responsibilities, and Resources*, developed by the ASAE & The Center Membership Council, 2008 ASAE & The Center for Association Leadership

dues revenue alone. How much would you spend to receive a $1,332 income stream? Fund your membership marketing with a view toward the lifetime value of a member.

4. Build your awareness of prospects by obtaining opt-ins.

Some associations have adopted the concept of "trading content for contact"—for example, offering a free article download or e-newsletter subscription in exchange for granting permission for further communication. These opt-ins are prime prospects for membership and can provide a high-response complement to outside list rentals.

5. Engage new members by encouraging a second interaction.

Survey data indicate that the more personal your follow-up interactions are with a new member, the more likely that member is to renew. Another key is to encourage additional interactions between the new member and your organization. For example, one organization's data showed that members who placed a product order in the past year were 28 percent more likely to renew than those who had not made a purchase. Eliciting almost any interaction from a new member, from having them complete a survey to simple phone contact, increases the likelihood of renewal.

6. Deploy multiple channels and higher frequency of contacts to renew members.
The days when three renewal notices got the job done are over. A renewal system today should include mail, email, and phone, with a total of 10 or more renewal contacts to achieve optimum returns.

7. Track and measure every membership marketing activity.
All the right membership marketing in the world will not make a difference without tracking. Even in well-run programs, the variance in results between the best and the worst marketing effort can be 1,000 percent or more, depending on timing, copy, lists, offers, and marketing channels. Carefully measuring results allows the proper allocation of marketing funds and best return for each dollar spent.[1]

8. Conduct a one-day pay-what-you-can membership promotion to gain new members.
Promote the drive to prospects who might not otherwise join but who will benefit from your member offerings. Promote your member opportunities such as discounted educational programs, and be sure to engage with these new members so that they'll pay full price when it's time to renew.

9. Try a member-get-a-member campaign.
But keep things easy. Send an email that can be forwarded.

10. Join, renew, register, purchase now and you'll be entered to win!
Boost your renewal rate, attendance, or sales, or attract new members with a drawing for the latest tech gadget. Use a promotional code that enters participants in the contest and allows you to track your campaign.

---

[1] Ideas 1-7 reprinted from "7 Proven Ways to Grow Your Membership," Tony Rossell, *Associations Now*, July 2010.

11. Contact your members with renewal messages early and often.

Start your renewal series early, add additional mailings, and email when memberships expire.

12. Tailor the renewal message to your acquisition message.

Is your message consistent across your marketing materials? Review your renewal copy to make sure you're reselling what members originally bought. This is especially important when converting new members toward the end of their first year.

13. Vary your package.

Redundant mailings are easy to ignore. Change the look of your mailer to get people to notice your message. This raises the cost slightly, but improved response rates will offset any increases.

14. Test methods.

Email, phone, and mail are all valid channels for renewals. If your organization sends an e-newsletter, add a renewal reminder during "expiration month." Stick reminder cards in your monthly magazine. Create a pop-up for users when they log in to the members section of your website. Make it hard for them to forget to renew.

15. Test packages.

While printing small quantities may drive up the cost of your renewal series, testing within your series is well worth the investment. Track by effort and by total response of the test and control groups. You'll want to select the methods and determine which ones drive the highest response for the least money.

16. Test offers.

Package tests keep the series fresh, whereas offer tests open up a world of possibilities. It doesn't have to be complicated. Early on in the series, try a long-term offer with a modest discount for a two-year commitment, with a fall-back offer of your standard one-year renewal.

17. Keep it simple.
With renewals and acquisitions, keep the offer simple. If it's too confusing—or if members perceive it as misleading—you'll get complaints instead of renewals.

18. Don't stop trying.
How many efforts should be in your renewal series? When do you stop? The rule of thumb is: "Keep mailing until response is no longer profitable." You should still tailor your messages.[2]

19. Use an automated message system to remind members to renew.
It may be less costly than your other follow-up methods. Calculate how many renewals you'd need to break even. Have a familiar staff member or volunteer record the message. Use the phone number (work, home, or cell) most likely to reach your members. Use a number that will show up in caller ID as your organization rather than an 800 number.

20. Hang onto members in tough economic times.
Consider offering a free one-time membership renewal to members who are unemployed when their membership is due to expire. You'll build good will, make it easier for them to pay for your other services, and may even help them land the job that enables them to pay for their renewal the next time around.

21. Lend a helping hand.
If you have an organizational membership model, allow members who are between jobs to access products and services at member rates for a period of time.

---

[2] Ideas 11-18 reprinted from "The Care and Feeding of Your Renewal Strategy," by Monica Williams, *Association Management*, June 2003.

Dues and Don'ts

22. Take a hard look at your dues structure.

When is the last time you increased dues? Have you added programs and services? It may be time to plan an increase.

23. If you must increase dues, effectively communicate the change to members.

Let them know early and often and don't rely on a single method of communication. As a guideline: Don't raise them by more than 10 percent without adding programs or services, and don't raise them by more than 20 percent without expecting to lose members and revenue.

24. Capture new dues with a new membership category.

Can you describe the group of individuals who attend your meetings, take your courses, and buy your products but don't join? If you can, you may be describing a new membership category. Look at whether or not you can provide them with a "home" within the organization, an attractive dues structure, and products and services that meet their needs, all while serving your mission. And be sure you consider the implications for governance and the possible effects on your current members.

25. Consider an opt-out strategy when combining renewal dues with a donation.

Your members may be more likely to make that donation when it's all totaled up neatly with their renewal than they are if they have to add it on themselves. Just be clear, make opting out easy, and expect a few squeaky wheels.

Cost to Serve a Member

Associations do not simply divide total operating costs by number of members to set dues. Doing so would probably make participation cost-prohibitive to many potential members. It is expected that nondues revenues will offset much of the operating expenses of an organization. However, at a minimum, the following costs should be included in the costs to serve a member:

1. Printing, production, and postage costs for the renewal series
2. Costs to produce, print, and mail membership publications/communications
3. Costs of membership staff—including salaries, benefits, and training
4. Technology and data processing costs for member service, such as T1 lines, call center equipment, and so forth
5. Web site expenses relating directly to membership
6. Research relating directly to membership, such as member needs or satisfaction surveys

Some organizations may want to include other costs such as:

1. Portion of rent, G&A, executive salaries, and technology expenses for the entire organization
2. Advocacy expenses
3. Communications and public awareness expenses
4. General research expenses
5. Revenue foregone from discounts extended to members for association events
6. General web site expenses

What does your cost to serve a member calculation help you do?

The cost of serving members is one of the important calculations in considering what your dues level should be. Whether or not to cover the full costs to serve a member is a basic philosophical decision to be made by the organization's leaders. If dues do not cover the costs to serve members, then additional products/services will need to be developed and sold to members to ensure the organization's continued financial viability.

continued on next page

continued from previous page

Calculating Costs to Serve Members

Cost to Serve Member	How to Calculate
Annual cost to serve a member	Yearly expenses divided by the number of members
Lifetime cost to serve a member	Annual cost to serve a member multiplied by the average tenure of membership

What should the relationship be between your dues income and your cost to serve members?

This will vary by organization and organization type—professional, trade, or philanthropic. A rule of thumb is that your cost-to-serve should be no more than 50 percent of your dues.

How often should your examine your cost to serve?

Cost to serve should be examined at least annually, usually during budget preparation time.

CAUTION

Cost-to-serve figures can swing widely depending on what expenses are loaded into the calculation. Be certain you have a good handle on what is truly related to serving members versus overhead calculations.

Reprinted from "Financial Metrics for the Membership Professional," by Susanne Connors Bowman and Lori Gusdorf, CAE, from *Membership Essentials: Recruitment, Retention, Roles, Responsibilities, and Resources*, developed by the ASAE & The Center Membership Council, 2008 ASAE & The Center for Association Leadership

26. Identify what your members need.

Members will pay for what they need and value. There are a number of ways to help identify members' needs including

- needs assessment surveys
- exit surveys
- focus groups
- competitive analysis
- collecting and tracking anecdotal feedback...

27. ...And offer it the right way.

In addition to offering exactly what members are looking for, you must also identify your audience and how to reach them. And don't skimp on the up-front analysis (see #35) needed to ensure that the product or service is duly differentiated from the competition and that the investment will be worth the forecast return.

28. Make sure the price is right.

Discuss what problems your profession faces that your association helps members resolve, and don't be afraid to charge what those products and services are worth.

29. Market, market, market.

Once you make the connection between what the association should be offering and what problems need resolutions, create a campaign that ties all the elements together.

30. Provide outstanding customer service.

It's worth the time and effort to make sure there's a live person answering the phone.

31. Know what your competition is offering.

There are always competitors aiming for a slice of your members' time, involvement, and money. You need to know where you stand in the market.[3]

---

[3] Ideas 26-31 reprinted from "6 Steps to Recruitment Success," by Summer Faust, *Associations Now*, September 2009.

32. Use training and certification programs to reach individual employees at member companies.

Design programs and certification below the CEO level to provide member benefits and cement your place in the industry.

33. When initiating a new nondues revenue program, consider running a pilot program before rolling it out to your entire membership.

Not only will you have an opportunity to gain and respond to valuable feedback, but you may also create a core of educated members who can spread the word.

34. Combine existing member programs to create packages.

A thorough review of your nondues revenue programs may reveal opportunities to combine offerings and promote them in new ways rather than create new programs.

35. Treat new nondues revenue programs like the businesses they are.

This means developing business plans and drawing upon staff or suppliers with the appropriate skills to conduct competitive analyses, forecasting, and financial analyses—for example, both before launch and on an ongoing basis.

36. Make yourself a match-maker.

Start a service to connect buyers with your members' valuable skills and knowledge.

37. Take your members on a trip.

Work with a travel company to offer your members a travel opportunity. Along with building community, a trip can provide your organization with a novel new revenue source.

38. Don't do it just for the sake of doing it.
Managing an affinity program takes time and effort. If that investment diverts resources away from serving your mission only to provide another credit card your members don't want or need, don't do it.

39. Know your members in order to develop an affinity program that benefits them and the work they do.
Use what you know to market your affinity programs effectively. The key to success is a customized approach.

40. Ensure that all direct mail pieces marketing your affinity program are cobranded.
This means making sure that any related direct mail pieces sent by your partner include your logo.

41. Make sure your members can learn about your affinity programs online.
Keep the online information short, simple, and easy to use, and give them a way to get in touch with a person if they have questions.

42. Gauge member awareness of affinity programs to decide what to promote and what to toss.
If an affinity program is performing poorly because of a lack of awareness, increase the marketing or give it higher placement on your website for a while. Streamline your affinity programs to include only those that provide your members with the most value. Ensure that you're increasing awareness and tracking participation.

43. Conduct webinars or other seminars that make experts and expert advice from your affinity partners available to your members.
For example, if you have an affinity insurance program, ask the supplier to sponsor a program in which it partners with an environmental consultant or law firm to offer risk-management tips.

ADVERTISING
AND
SPONSORSHIP

The Care and Feeding of Corporate Relationships

44. Don't be haphazard.
Establish a process for finding and maintaining corporate sponsors to keep the money flowing.

45. Cultivate corporate relationships.
Show your corporate partners that you know your industry and can articulate opportunities that offer mutual benefits.

46. Keep your sponsors happy.
Make them feel welcome at events by greeting them personally. Streamline sponsorship opportunities into packages and centralize the point of communication. Offer incentives like priority-point systems that reward companies for repeated and consistent support.

47. Ensure a successful partnership.

Deliver what you promise. Adjust to each sponsor's needs. Don't overlook small companies. Keep sponsors up to date. Consider working with a consulting firm to manage sponsorship efforts if you don't have enough capacity in house. Be selective in soliciting sponsorships.

48. Thank your sponsors publicly.

Make them feel appreciated and raise their visibility by thanking them by name and logo. Visibility is a big part of what they're paying for, so get creative to show you're making an effort to give them their money's worth.

Opportunities for Visibility and Engagement

49. Sing their names from the rooftops.

Allow sponsors to place product ads on aisle banners in your exhibit hall. If you have aisle banners listing booth numbers, place product ads under the numbers.

50. Find novel spaces.

Allow sponsors of information booths or internet stations to promote their products in space around the computer screens.

51. Innovate when it comes to interaction.

Find ways sponsors can interact directly with your members. Be open to sponsors' ideas about how they might engage with your audience. If necessary, create categories of sponsorship, e.g., those that allow mention of a specific product and those that allow only promotion of corporate names.

52. Engage the audience on the sponsors' behalf.

Consider these ideas: Involve the sponsors' charity; integrate the sponsors' message or theme into activities; or, schedule sponsor experts to participate in round-table discussions that give valuable takeaways for the attendees.

53. If you have a publication—in print or online—that is published without a sponsor or advertising, ask whether it's published that way because neither sponsorship nor advertising is permitted or because neither has ever been offered.

Even when there's a policy against product advertising, there may be room for sponsorship. If sponsorship is a possibility, add the publication to your sponsorship brochure and packages, put the word out to your corporate partners or members, and treat it like you would any other sponsorship opportunity.

54. Use a vendor to provide your members with hard-to-find, up-to-the-minute industry information.

If you're having a hard time scooping the competition with your weekly e-newsletters, consider working with a vendor who can provide better, more frequent information—as well as a valuable sponsorship opportunity.

55. Use care when giving recognition to corporate donors.

When recognition becomes "advertising," you may be jeopardizing the tax-free treatment of the contribution. Know the IRS rules that cover the differentiation of an "acknowledgment" from "advertising."

Making the Most of Advertising

56. Take a hard look at your advertising sales program.

Compare it to your competitors', identify target markets, and set competitive ad rates. Know your share of the market. Review the structure of your program to ensure that your contact methods are effective. Provide an editorial calendar on which a tactical marketing plan can be based. Review cross-selling opportunities and let advertisers know how these opportunities help them reach their target market. Help your advertisers develop integrated marketing approaches to your audience that include print, online, and other opportunities to get their messages across.

57. Use market research to sell more ads.

Do potential advertisers really understand who your audience is—including characteristics such as their buying power—and what your publications provide to them? If your magazine isn't stacking up against the competition when it comes to ad sales, ask the prospective advertisers. If there are misconceptions, conduct reader research to refute those misconceptions.

58. Leverage member demographics to attract corporate money.

Your organization might not have anything to do with luxury products like cars and travel, but if your members' demographics are attractive to the people who sell luxury cars and travel, you might find new sources of advertising and sponsorship. Take a look at who your members are and think about what they might buy or do that has nothing to do with you. Think about who might want to reach them, and make the ask.

59. Don't waste prime advertising space.

The inside front cover and first page, middle spread of a saddle-stitched publication, last page, and inside and outside back cover are premium ad spaces and should be sold that way. If you're using one of those spaces to promote your own meetings and events every month and relegating paid advertisements to other parts of the book, you're losing money. And by the way, charge a premium for those ad positions.

60. Don't go digital.

At least not without evaluating its potential effect on ad revenue. If you're heavily reliant on print advertising, consider a digital edition that includes advertising and start marketing it to your advertisers. Come up with creative ways to encourage uptake—without giving away advertising—and reap the benefits of both worlds.

61. Try an auction.

Auction advertising space in your association's magazine to attract new advertisers and stand out from the crowd. Set a reserve price, then publish and publicize the auction terms.

Consider Video Advertising

Vendors often ask associations if they can sponsor educational sessions at a conference. For most, the answer is a resounding no. With a little creative thinking, however, there are opportunities. One association that had a strict policy came up with the idea of not allowing the session to be sponsored but allowing the video recording of the session to be sponsored. The exhibitor picked three sessions from the conference that perfectly matched its product suite and paid $15,000 to sponsor the recordings. In return, the sponsor received a 10-second video advertisement that was played before the online session playback for three months. The cost to the association to have the sessions recorded by its A/V vendor was approximately $6,000. The net revenue from this simple example was $9,000, with little effort required from the association.

Reprinted from *Social Networking for Nonprofits: Increasing Engagement in a Mobile and Web 2.0 World,* by Andy Steggles, 2010 ASAE & The Center for Association Leadership

62. Sell banner or other advertising space in HTML email digests of email list or forum postings and discussions.

At a rate of 10 cents per email generated, a daily digest sent out five days per week to a list of 10,000 subscribers could generate $5,000 per week.

63. For subtlety, try text.

Not text message ads, but a line or two of text advertising at the bottom of non-HTML emails such as alerts that let subscribers know a new issue of your journal has just been published.

MEETINGS AND EXPOS

64. Change the name of your annual event to attract attendees.

Make the name more exciting and inviting to stand out and show that you're doing things differently.

65. Hold a hosted-buyer event.

The hosted-buyer model tweaks the traditional tradeshow format with the intention of providing more motivated buyers and therefore more qualified sales leads for exhibitors. In a hosted-buyer show, attendees must apply to attend, proving their qualifications as a buyer in the industry. Those who are selected to become hosted buyers have some or all of their expenses, including airfare, hotel, and food, paid by the show. Exhibitor fees are used to cover the costs of the hosted buyers. Buyers benefit from reduced costs, while exhibitors benefit from access to buyers who have proven their qualifications as purchasers. Hosted-buyer shows often provide opportunities for buyers to make appointments with sellers for specific meeting times prior to the show. Hosted buyers may be required to make a certain number of appointments during the show.

66. Add an appointment show to your traditional trade show.
Make your show more valuable to both attendees and exhibitors by giving them an opportunity to schedule face time that won't involve wrestling through a crowd to be seen and heard.

67. Put your pressroom to work.
Consider selling sponsorship of your pressroom or renting out space for private press conferences.

68. Boost your meeting attendance with hybrid conferencing technology.
Expand the reach of your meeting to people who are not able to attend in person by using conference technology that provides a live stream to online attendees, who can watch and even participate in real time.

A Boost from Booths

69. Design booth packages.
Chances are the bulk of your exhibitors' expenses are in logistics, shipping, and setup. You can raise your revenue and help them save at the same time if you can offer customized booths that they won't need to ship or assemble.

70. Charge a premium for desirable booth positions.
Rather than price each booth space the same, determine the best positions (e.g., near the entrance) and charge more for them.

71. Don't wait until the show's over to start selling space.
Take the time during your tradeshow to visit exhibitors and get the ball rolling on signing them up for the following year.

72. Start selling next year's show even before this year's begins.

Then, when your show starts, work with exhibitors who have made a commitment to help them make their booth selection for the following year.

73. Marketing to exhibitors is still marketing.

Know your audience. Know your competition. Develop your brand. Keep them informed. Grow the relationships.

Keep Costs Under Control

74. If you're anticipating lower attendance at a meeting, talk to the hotel about renegotiating terms.

A hotel would probably rather have you there for a smaller meeting than have you cancel altogether. You may be able to reduce your room and food and beverage commitments.

75. Cut your tradeshow or educational program down to one day.

With travel budgets slashed and schedules tight as ever, people may be more likely to attend a shorter meeting, especially if they can get away without a hotel stay.

76. Manage currency fluctuations to keep international meetings profitable.

Consider purchasing currency at a set rate ahead of the meeting, paying some expenses in advance, setting up a local bank account, paying expenses in local currency, and keeping exchanges to a minimum.

77. Don't waste coffee.

To reduce expenses for coffee service during meetings, request that the hotel/venue provide teacups and saucers instead of mugs. Mugs are more likely to be left half full.

78. Drop the reception in favor of Riesling and Roquefort.

Instead of offering a welcome reception during meeting events, kick off with a wine and cheese party. It sounds just as elegant as a reception, but attendees will eat and drink much less. Attendees will not arrive expecting a stand-in for a meal.

79. Negotiate facilitator or instructor fees on a sliding scale based on actual attendance.

Most would rather accept a 25 percent reduction in their normal fee than have 100 percent of nothing if the class or presentation has to be canceled because of low registration numbers. This also encourages the facilitator or instructor to assist with the marketing.

80. Make your convention daily pay for itself or generate a profit.

If one or two sponsorships are not enough to cover the cost of your convention publication, consider opening it to advertising instead. Consider a set inventory of advertising space in the daily to generate demand and manage your costs.

81. Keep distribution costs of convention publications under control.

Room drops can be expensive. Consider negotiating the price with your hotels or taking an alternative route. Use stands or staff at entrances, in lobbies, at information desks, and in break areas.

82. Work with a destination management company.

Outsourcing some or all of your event planning, management, or logistics to a company with local expertise, connections, and staff can save you time and money, manage your risk, and maybe even give you an "in" at special venues that will make your meetings more memorable.

83. Control the bottom line by making cuts no one will notice.

Does anyone really pay attention to decorations? Are they talking about all the bells and whistles in the staging of that keynote or award presentation? Will they complain about a more limited food and beverage selection?

Minimize Attrition

84. Educate members about attrition fees that can result when attendees book outside of the room block.

85. Provide incentives for booking within the room block.

86. Know companies' official reservation policies to better plan your booking.

87. Package discounted registration and hotel booking and shorten the lead time.

88. Focus promotion on longer-tenured and loyal members, who are more likely to book within the block.

89. Take steps to prevent room-block pirates from luring your attendees into room blocks that aren't yours.

WEBSITES, SOCIAL MEDIA, AND MORE

90. Bring search marketing home.

To capture some of the dollars big advertisers are now spending with the large search engines, consider offering search-driven advertising on your own site. To increase your site's search value, consider opening up more of your content to nonmembers—for example, make magazine articles free after a year and open up access to online discussions, questions, answers, blogs, comments, and responses.

91. Conduct an online auction to turn donated goods into revenue.

Check out the opportunities on eBay and the many smaller auction sites, or run a virtual auction on your own website. Take advantage of free marketing tools at eBay's Giving Works program or use its MissionFish service, both of which are geared toward fundraising for nonprofits. Get the word out, and make it easy for people to bid by offering options.

92. Build an online job bank to attract visitors, build interest, and generate nondues revenue.

Keep it open to the public to allow employers and recruiters to reach as many candidates as possible. If you don't have the capacity in house to sell and maintain job bank listings, consider working with a vendor.

93. Expand your exhibit hall onto your website.

But follow these guidelines to make sure your virtual trade show falls within safe harbor and will not be subject to UBIT: Make your online show "ancillary" to your in-person trade show. Be sure your online content will "augment and enhance" the in-person show by making available "in an alternative medium the same information available at the show." Make your web-based show available only "during essentially the same limited time period that each [live] trade show is in operation."

94. Leverage your website to go global.

Identify like organizations abroad whose members might be interested in your programs and activities. Form agreements that provide those organizations' members access to your member-only online content while providing you with a new revenue stream.

95. Get a Google Grant.

Many nonprofit organizations, especially those with a focus on health-related issues, should make every effort to secure a Google grant. Having a Google grant—worth approximately $300 a month in advertising on Google.com—allows you to participate in the Google AdWords program, where you can create targeted ads based on key words. For example, you can create an ad saying "shop online and fight [insert disease]. Get amazing gifts & support a great cause. [insert your organization's URL]." As long as you actively manage the account, you will continue to remain in the Google Grants program. There is no end date for your grant and no need to re-apply at any time.

Analyzing Your Revenue

Before getting down to assessing how your online presence can best support your overall revenue, you need to know a few key details about how your organization generates cash. Here are some ideas to get you started:

- Identify the programs, services and other revenue sources that generate a significant majority of the organization's income.
- For those revenue sources, determine what percentage currently comes in via the web vs. other sources.
- Determine the expense of receiving that revenue via e-commerce versus the mail or other methods.
- With that data in hand, discuss the following:
  - What brings in the most revenue online?
  - What brings in the least?
  - Is revenue received online more profitable?
  - Which program or service is the most amenable to online revenue collection? Which is the least?

Conducting the analysis above will help you to understand how money flows into your organization, the current role your site has in that flow, and how you may want to change that over time to increase gross revenue and total profits. This knowledge will be invaluable as you consider which of the revenue strategies in this chapter are most relevant to your goals and what you should be trying to achieve online.

Reprinted from *Online and On Mission: Practical Web Strategy for Breakthrough Results*, by C. David Gammel, CAE, 2009 ASAE & The Center for Association Leadership

96. Put join/give/volunteer on center stage.

You don't need to put all the details on your homepage, but do make the link stand out. Potential members, donors, and volunteers who find your homepage via a link in a Tweet, on a blog, or on Facebook are more likely to become actual members, donors, and volunteers if you make it easy for them to get the information they need.

97. Boost your campaign with a PURL.

A personalized URL built from a prospect's name or customized for a campaign takes a respondent onto a specialized page. Content can be customized and personalized for the prospect and the campaign.

98. Make it easy for people to pay you.

Whether it's your conference registration site, membership application or renewal, or online store, the easier you make it for people to complete their order and check out, the more likely you are to keep the order. Take the time to act like a customer every once in a while to see where there's room for improvement. Walk through the entire process and see which parts take the most time, require you to re-do actions, or simply aren't clear. Take a look at your website's stats to find out how many people abandon the online ordering process and where to identify hang-ups that you might have breezed past.

99. Make your online publication complement your print version.

Take advantage of the online medium to provide things you can't in print: expanded stories, additional information, multimedia presentations... And don't forget the ads. Add value for your advertisers with links and other online extras.

100. Check out the merchandise.

To get ideas for what to stock in your online or meeting store, take a look at the competition. What are similar organizations offering—and what are they trying to get rid of? But don't stop there. Stay up on what's hot in retail. What's the latest must-have for people who share your audience's demographics?

Social Media Savvy

101. Build and engage your Twitter communities before you ask for support and funds.

Don't make your first Tweet a request for money. Build a following and engage people; then be careful how you word the ask.

102. On Facebook, keep your fan page activities separate from fundraising.

Use the fan page to share news and information, but use a cause page to solicit donations.

103. Don't re-create the wheel.

Explore pre-built online community software and hosting solutions before you embark on a more costly custom project.

104. Mine social media for stories.

It's no longer enough to use canned content for a donation request. You need to have a compelling story. Identify people who are active on your message boards or in the various social media presences of your organization. Get to know them and learn their stories. Once you've built a rapport, get permission to share their stories. You can craft a donation ask around someone who has been living with an illness for several years. Or for a different spin, create a request around the story of a caregiver. Share that perspective so when your constituents get your enewsletter or direct mail piece, they may see themselves in that personal story and be willing to support your cause, whether it's with a donation, a purchase, or a membership application.

105. Use the Causes Application on Facebook.

If you're a nonprofit, take advantage of the Causes Application on Facebook. You can use the Causes application as an online fundraising arm for your organization and as an action center. Keep the folks who join your cause engaged by pushing content to them: Tell them the latest news from your organization. Let them know about upcoming events, like walks or web chats. Perhaps your organization has a monthly magazine and you're trying to recruit potential interviewees for specific articles; use Causes. Keeping your Cause active and your constituents engaged will increase your donations via the application.

106. Use social media outlets to drive readers to your website.

LinkedIn, Facebook, Twitter, and other social media outlets are not replacements for your website—at least not yet! Use them like the complementary tools they are, keep them social, go light on text, and link back to let your website do the heavy lifting.

Leveraging eGroups
(Discussion Groups/Listservers/Forums)

Many associations already provide some kind of listserver as a member benefit. Listservers tend to have a love/hate relationship with association members. Members get frustrated with the "digest within a digest" issues from people replying to a single email in a digest but forgetting to remove the rest of the digest. Poor subject-line descriptions from people replying to the digest without changing the subject line are also a nuisance. Embarrassing emails sent to the entire listserver instead of the individual person, spam, out-of-office messages, and so on also cause concern. Over the years, some associations tried to address these issues by moving to online forums. This was usually not successful because the forums were not as proactive as the listservers; they did not typically send email digests. Many associations that moved to forums, saw a sudden drop in traffic because the assumption that readers would visit the website every day to view the content was flawed.

Consequently, a compromise of the traditional, proactive listservers with the high functionality, web-based forums was created. eGroups operate like listservers except for some key features. One of them is the fact that the emails generated are HTML-based so they actually look like webpages that are delivered by email. Essentially you are delivering emails in the same format as the email newsletters that you may already be sending out. If this is the case, why not embed advertising in these emails as well? That is what a number of associations are now doing. Every time a member posts a message, the emails that are sent out to the membership at large contain subtle, nonintrusive sponsorship or advertising. No longer do you need to wait another month or two before the next newsletter is ready; you can now generate new revenue every day.

When launching eGroups, a best practice is to avoid putting advertising or sponsorship in the email to start with, but instead to use the ad space to promote your own products and services. Once members are used to the new format and the embedded ads for your own products, then slowly start replacing them with ads. By the time you do this, vendors likely will have contacted you asking about this new opportunity.

So how much do you charge for this new ad medium? A simple answer is to look at how much you charge for advertising in your newsletters if they are targeted to the same group. Models for charging differ based on the frequency of postings and the size of the egroup.

continued from previous page

For example, if you have a group of 2,000 people in a single community and the eGroup is fairly active, with messages posted an average of five days per week, then you might want to consider charging 10¢ per subscriber, per day. In this instance, one week's advertising would work out to be:

$0.10 (10¢) × 2,000 (subscribers) = $200 per day

$200 × 5 (days) = $1,000 per week in new revenue

Calculated over an entire year, the potential nondues revenue is impressive.

If you had a community of 500 people that was not very active and had only one or two postings every other week, then you might want to take a different approach to selling advertising. It is difficult to charge per week or for any short time when the frequency of postings is so limited. For smaller or more targeted eGroups you could adopt a flat fee over a longer time, using historical data to "guess-timate" (with no guarantee) how many messages will be generated. In this example, you might work out something like the following:

Two messages every other week = approximately five messages per month, 30 messages per six months or 60 messages per year.

$0.10 (10¢) × 500 (subscribers) = $50 per day

$50 × 30 (days where there is at least one message) = $1,500 for a six-month sponsorship

There are different pricing models, including pay-per-click or per opened email. Of course, not everyone charges 10 cents per subscriber either; some charge more or less, depending on the perceived value of the eGroup. Consider this: If you were a vendor trying to sell to one of ASAE's listservers, such as Technology, Marketing, Finance, or Executive, how much would you pay for access to these specific market segments?

If your association does not have the resources to sell this new type of offering, consider outsourcing the sales to a third party. Normally, there is a split, or at least a commission, of revenue on anything they sell, but it is still better than nothing. To see an example of eGroup message with embedded advertisement, go to http://bit.ly/egroupexample.

Reprinted from *Social Networking for Nonprofits: Increasing Engagement in a Mobile and Web 2.0 World,* by Andy Steggles, 2010 ASAE & The Center for Association Leadership

Satisfy Your Mobile Members

107. Look to mobile technology to provide new ways to connect to and serve your members:

108. Membership applications—
Provide a "mobile lite" version of your membership application and reduce it from a five-page document to a half-page one. Get a prospective member's name, address, and basic demographic information—enough to decide his or her likely viability to be accepted as a member. Collect any further information after you've received the provisional application and money. This can increase the number of completed applications from those who might give up on an overly complex form.

109. Industry news—
Rather than updating members daily or weekly, do it continuously with a constant stream of updated news. For example, let's say you hire a news-clipping service to produce abstracts of the top-40 articles of the day affecting your industry. With a mobile application, articles can be uploaded throughout the day, and every time a member checks for "latest news," he or she will likely see more content. A daily email version can still go out to those who want it, of course, but those who like to keep their fingers on the pulse will connect the association by receiving the latest information.

110. Career center—
The most frequently visited portion of an association website is often the job bank. Why not have a career-center mobile application? It could be as simple as an RSS feed that sends the latest job postings to members via the mobile application.

111. Member directories—
Upgrade the directory's functionality so that it becomes a full-fledged professional social network. Use an application that allows members to find colleagues with similar interests, "friend" each other, and view richer, more informative profiles.

112. Discussion groups—

Usually one of an association's most popular member benefits is its discussion groups and listservers. Consider creating a mobile application that will allow members to post questions or responses, view author profiles, and connect with fellow members.

113. Facebook, Twitter, and LinkedIn integration—

Social media tools offer tremendous mobile-app opportunities. For example, if your organization has a Facebook page, create an application that allows members to write on your Wall or upload photos or videos. This is a simple way of generating engagement from chapter meetings or industry events. Every member can be a content provider if you make access easy enough.

114. Events—

A variety of mobile applications can be developed around your events. Online registration is the most obvious possibility, but you can be even more creative. For instance, the American College of Cardiology recently released a mobile exhibitor directory application. Another area of opportunity is sponsorship. Why not include paid ads?[1]

---

[1] Ideas 108-114 reprinted from "Serve Your Mission With Mobile Technology," *Associations Now,* July 2010.

OPERATIONS

115. Evaluate any action that might save the organization money in light of its potential effect on member value.

If that cost-saving solution affects your ability to serve members or your mission, it might cost more than you think.

116. Cut, or cut back, out-of-date programs.

If there is an outcry by individuals who are emotionally attached to a program that is behind the times and the books, ask if they're willing to completely defray the cost of continuing it. If they're not, cut your losses.

117. Reduce or eliminate payments for board member travel.

If there's a policy that requires paying for it, find ways to cut back on the amount of travel or the costs. Let them fly coach!

118. Don't keep your staff in the dark.

When it comes to focusing on the net of an event or program, staff members need to understand the importance of budgeting well and managing expenses, and they should be given opportunities and encouragement for coming up with cost-saving ideas.

119. Reward staff for suggesting and implementing cost-saving measures.

Make it systematic. Create a vehicle for staff to submit their ideas and a body for evaluating their suggestions. At a set period of time after a suggestion is adopted, evaluate the actual savings. If savings have been achieved, reward the staff member(s) who made the suggestion with a bonus equal to a percentage of the savings.

120. Renegotiate your lease.

There's no harm in asking, but do your homework first: Learn about the local market, including the vacancy rate and rents for spaces similar to yours. Determine whether you'd be willing to move within the building to a smaller or less-visible space. Figure out what other items might be negotiable, such as maintenance fees.

121. Co-locate with another association.

Extra office space after a move or downsizing? Consider seeking another association to sublease. Know your terms, envision the potential benefits such as the opportunity for partnerships and collaboration, be flexible, and make sure your staff members know what's happening.

122. Make a move.

Whether you're outgrowing your offices or starting to hear echoes, a move could be an opportunity to save or even make some money. Just be sure to factor in all of the costs, both direct, such as moving expenses, and indirect, such as staff down-time.

123. Buy meeting supplies on location.

Save the money you would spend on shipping by shopping around ahead of time and arranging to purchase supplies at your destination.

124. Bring exhibit sales in house.

If you're paying a consultant or outside firm a commission to sell space to the same companies every year, you may be able to increase your net income by handling those sales in house.

125. Assess inventory levels on a regular basis.

Regularly assess inventory levels of products, such as publications, that you are selling. Backorders cost money when you have to process two packages and incur shipping fees twice. On the flip side, carry too much inventory and you might find you're paying for storage that is over and above what you saved by printing a large quantity. And by all means, be sure to evaluate the inventory that is not moving. You could be paying more to store inventory than it would cost you to write it off.

126. Get on a predictable schedule for hardware replacements.

Knowing when you'll need to upgrade servers, desktops, laptops, backup systems, and other IT hardware will allow you to budget accordingly and avoid surprises.

127. Evaluate your distribution channels.

Which are operating well, and which are underperforming? Take a look at the underperformers to see where you can make improvements. If you've done everything you can but the channel is still a trickle, see what it's costing you. If it's costing more than it's bringing in, close it off.

128. Use telecommuting to save on space.

Create shared workspaces, or "hotels," for employees who telecommute regularly.

129. Ditch your fax machine.

Start using an e-fax system instead of an old-fashioned fax machine. E-faxes may be distributed electronically (reducing administrative processing) and stored electronically. The cost of the e-fax subscription will probably be less than the dedicated phone line.

130. Merge to succeed.

Ask yourself whether merging with a related organization might help both organizations save—and make—money. Consider the following possibilities: consolidation of duplicate programs; better value to members and customers through combined services, networks, and reach; market expansion; and savings through "economies of scale, reduction of overhead, elimination of nonessential functions, or incorporation of new or improved business processes or procedures."

131. Manage energy costs and efficiencies.
Explore your alternatives for purchasing gas or electricity for your building. There may be a cheaper source.

132. Go digital for record retention.
Reducing those boxes and boxes of records down to byte-sized pieces could save you a bundle on warehousing and storage fees. Just make sure the cost of scanning, organizing, and archiving all those paper documents doesn't cost you more than you'll save.

133. Retain your employees.
Know what it's going to cost to hire and train a new employee and weigh that against what it might cost you to retain one in whom you've already made an investment.

Manage Production and Fulfillment Costs

134. Make it brief.
To avoid multiple and potentially costly rounds of design and proofing changes, institute a process in which internal customers must provide marketing and production staff with a creative brief outlining each project, be it a brochure or a t-shirt. Follow it up with a meeting in which marketing and the client make sure they're on the same page about the product, the audience, and the objectives.

135. Know what change is going to cost you.
For each design or production project, get a bid that indicates the number of comps that will be provided, the number of rounds of proofs included, and itemized charges for exceeding those numbers.

136. Be sure the vendor fits.
Even your favorite printer's repeat customer pricing might not be the best you can do if they only have a sheet-fed press and the quantity

and format of your job is better suited to a web press—or vice versa. Know your vendors' capabilities and limits to make the best match.

137. It never hurts to ask.
Don't be shy about requesting discounts for volume or repeat business from your design and production vendors. You'll be no worse off if the answer is no, and you might get a clue that it's time to shop around a bit.

138. Consider a vendor's location.
If you're in one of the more expensive parts of the country and you're only using local shops, consider looking at vendors in places where the cost of living is lower. Don't just hit the yellow web pages. Get some word-of-mouth recommendations from far-flung colleagues, and give the companies who sound promising an opportunity to bid on your next project.

139. Keep track of savings, not only costs.
By documenting how much you're saving on each project by virtue of your vendor selection, discounts, or adjustments to the way a project is done, you'll give yourself an opportunity to see patterns. If savings are consistently high with a certain production method, for example, you'll know to consider it first, which will save you both time and money.

140. Invest in print management software.
Some systems do a lot more than just capture details about each job, from sending out requests for quotes to allowing potential vendors to enter quotes directly into the database. All that data can be output into charts that allow you to make cost comparisons quickly and easily.

141. Give suppliers an opportunity to earn and keep your business.
Go beyond the quote by telling them what you need and what you want to spend. A vendor who wants your business is going to work with you to get there. You may not want to take the suggestion to trim down the size or use two colors instead of four, for example,

but at the very least you'll learn something that might help you save money on the next job.

142. Go digital—digital printing, that is.
For small jobs a digital press may be the most cost-effective solution, and these days, it's getting harder and harder to tell the difference between pieces printed digitally and those produced on traditional presses.

143. Consider a redesign.
If your publication is getting old and stale, ask yourself whether a redesign might help you serve a membership with changing demographics, attract new members, or provide better opportunities for advertising sales.

144. Drop the print.
An electronic newsletter can be more timely, more frequent, and more trackable, as well as more cost efficient, than a print newsletter.

145. Partner up to stock your photo files.
Work with an organization in the same industry to set up a photo shoot. Share the cost and reap the savings.

146. Bring design in house.
If you're paying suppliers to design your publications, marketing pieces, and web pages and at the same time you have a person on staff to execute those designs in your magazine, for example, consider drawing on that staff person's expertise or hiring someone with more design experience who can do both the creative work and redesigns and the day-to-day layout. It's not the best solution for every organization, but for some and under the right circumstances, it can result in cost savings and greater flexibility to make changes.

147. Gang like orders.
If you need to print multiple versions of a piece for various field offices, provide a cut-off date for versions and gang the orders together. You'll see a much lower cost per unit and can just drop ship all at once.

148. Calculate annual usage for materials and order accordingly.

You can save quite a bit when printing or ordering more at one time. So for materials that you know will remain static, go ahead and order a year or two worth of stock and fulfill from that stock. You can store at your own warehouse/fulfillment center or work out a deal with your vendor to manage this inventory for you (some won't even charge for this service).

149. Do your homework to ensure that international mailings are successful and cost effective.

Give your communications a local look: Match the culture and feel of the destination and include a locally addressed, postage-paid reply envelope. Know the transportation modes and service standards for local delivery; prepare mailings with the ultimate delivery date in mind. Familiarize yourself with local mail customs and best practices.

Go Green

150. Go green to save some green.

Upgrading your building to be more energy efficient can take a significant investment, but some changes, such as upgraded lighting, may pay for themselves in savings in as little as three years.

151. Provide reusable coffee cups and water bottles to reduce consumption of paper products and cut down on the amount of solid waste you produce.

152. Turn out the lights to save electricity.

153. Encourage paperless workflows to save paper and waste.

154. Provide incentives for taking public transportation or biking to work; pay for fewer parking spaces.

155. Return toner and printer cartridges for recycling rebates.

156. Print and copy double sided to save paper.

157. Change the default margins in Microsoft Word to 0.75 inches or less to use less paper.

158. Purchase used or refurbished equipment to save money and keep it out of a landfill.

Keep Cash Flowing

159. Raise the amount of the required deposit on the sale of exhibit space.
When exhibitors commit and pay their deposits, you're assured of the revenue.

160. Require payment up front.
It will improve your cash flow and allow staff to devote time to something other than collections.

161. Adopt a rolling membership year.
Your cash flow and the burden of invoicing and receiving renewals will be spread out over 12 months rather than all lumped together.

162. Collect your money!
Just because your corporate members are paying many thousands of dollars doesn't mean you should let their renewals slide. In fact, that's even more reason to invest in the time and effort of making a personal reminder phone call.

Budgeting and Accounting

163. Know your numbers.
It's impossible to make sound decisions if you don't know the state of your finances. Taking the time now to project cash flow, analyze the costs of programs, and understand your credit situation may save you money if you have to make quick decisions later.

164. Know how much you should be spending.

Invest in an operating ratio report that covers associations similar to yours. You'll have a valuable source of benchmarks against which to compare your own budgets.

165. Ensure that income is categorized correctly.

Not knowing the difference between a licensing fee and a royalty, or between advertising and sponsorship, could cost you. Having a handle on your unrelated business income is key to managing your tax burden and avoiding fines.

166. Adopt yearly membership that coincides with your fiscal year.

With a small staff, less technological capacity, and a small membership, it may be more manageable than a rolling system and may facilitate dues planning and budgeting.

167. Make the switch to program-based budgeting.

If you're currently budgeting on a departmental or functional basis, making the switch to a process that assigns both revenues and costs (all costs) to programs will help you better know the true cost of a given program and make better decisions about which programs to keep and which to cut.

168. When evaluating a program's financial performance, don't forget the cost of staff support.

Programs that generate significant revenue may require specialized staff support and therefore higher labor costs. An offering that looks great in terms of the dollars it's bringing in to the association may not look as good when you factor in the amount of time or the type of staff necessary to administer it.

169. Pass a "shadow" budget that shows what will be done in case revenues are higher or lower than expected.

Assigning priority to what activities will be added or cut will allow the organization to react quickly without jeopardizing essential programs.

Price It Right

170. Consider both direct and indirect costs when reviewing the pricing of products and services.

Although you may be looking at overhead on a larger scale when you prepare financial statements and 990s, try allocating those indirect costs on a product-by-product basis. You may find you've been selling some of them at a loss without knowing it.

171. Make sure you're charging enough for shipping and handling.

Consider both direct and indirect costs, and think about building in a small profit. Above all, make sure you're not losing money.

172. Switch to a managed services plan for IT.

A support plan that works on a fixed-price rather than by the hour can help you control ongoing support costs.

Manage Risk

173. Plan for business continuity.

Crisis-management planning should involve four phases: preparation, prevention, response, and recovery. A sound plan can keep a crisis from turning into a disaster.

174. Have a written investment policy.

Written guidelines, goals, and strategies will help you evaluate your position and plan your response to a volatile market.

175. Ensure that your reserve fund is protected.

Know the FDIC individual deposit insurance limits and be sure you understand them as they apply to your accounts. Consider spreading your funds among several banks to stay below the limits.

MARKETING

176. Brand does not live by logo alone.
Strong branding comes from more than a consistent logo and color scheme or tagline. It comes from using every opportunity to tell the story of what you do.

177. Discount, discount, discount.
If you're pricing things appropriately, you can afford to offer discounts to drive up sales, membership, renewals, registration, etc. Try various discounts in your marketing pieces and track results to better understand what your audience is willing to pay.

178. In an economic downturn, don't do prospect mailings.
If you can't help yourself, do small test mailings with highly targeted groups, and keep your costs down.

179. Use templates to create custom but consistent messages.
Web-based templates and digital print on demand make it easy to provide your chapters, field offices, or affiliates with well-branded but highly customized promotional pieces or programmatic material.

180. Conduct cross-media campaigns.
In a cross-media campaign you're putting your magazine, website, social media outlets, email, and direct mail to work in a coordinated effort to raise funds, increase attendance, gain new members. Track responses via each channel so that you can evaluate your results.

181. Track your efforts.

With no tracking, every marketing piece you do will be a test with no results. Take some of the guesswork out by using promotional codes, personalized URLs (PURLs), and web analytics so that you can follow up on success and drop the things that aren't working.

182. Don't just personalize; customize.

In the digital world and its extension, print on demand, you can do more than just change names and addresses. Go a step further and use variable data printing to customize content, adding a personal touch to your campaign. More often than not, the additional cost is offset by a higher response rate.

183. Make sure your launch of a new product, service, or initiative doesn't get lost at your annual meeting.

Put extra effort into planning ways to cut through the noise or consider different timing. Treat meeting launches as part of a larger effort. Build pre-meeting buzz, then be sure to follow up afterward.

Marketing Pitfalls to Avoid

Several pitfalls commonly plague a strategic marketing plan. Avoid a plan that

- **Lists only goals, not strategies.** Such plans often fail to support assumptions with factual research.

- **Lacks support from the top.** Adequate resources have not been allocated to make the plan work. Perhaps the person in charge of the planning process has not been given sufficient authority to move ahead or lacks support staff.

- **Disenfranchises staff.** Even if the marketing planning process is a centralized effort, staff from every department must provide input and support. A sound centralized function is open and embraces coordination and facilitation. Every staff member has some responsibility for marketing, regardless of association size.

- **Is based on flawed assumptions.** A good marketing plan must be more than a wish list or goal statement. Successful plans contain information about how conclusions were derived. Financial data should not be accepted without supporting information as to how and on what basis assumptions were drawn.

- **Relies on poor-quality market research.** Some staff leaders fall into the trap of believing that market research will be too costly or take up too much time. Associations must be willing to commit to ongoing, quality market research. Remember the old saying: No research is better than bad research.

- **Is not comprehensive.** If a plan is developed for a one-time event or opportunity, it may do more harm than good. The plan must be integrated with all the activities of the association.

- **Gives no one the responsibility for marketing planning.** Another old saying to keep in mind: If everyone is in charge, no one is in charge.

Reprinted from *Professional Practices in Association Management, Second Edition,* chapter by Alan R. Shark, CAE, 2007 ASAE & The Center for Association Leadership

FUNDRAISING

184. Ask! Don't overlook any prospects.

Research documented in *The Decision to Give* (ASAE: The Center for Association Leadership, 2010) points out that 80 percent of members who have never given, beyond dues, report that they have never been asked. Yet they are satisfied with their membership and give to other causes, making them viable prospects for donating to their association or its related foundation.

185. Match your list.

Analyze your donor list and then look for other lists with matching demographics in order to target your prospecting.

186. Build your capacity to attract and serve prospective donors of diverse backgrounds.

If you confine yourself to homogeneity, you're limiting your funding pool and ignoring a world of possibilities.

187. Get more bang for your fundraising buck.

Focus on less expensive fundraising methods and cultivate donors with a known connection to your organization or cause. Increase your activities in major gifts, planned gifts, online solicitations, and corporate and foundation grants. Cut back on direct mail, telephone, and special-event fundraising programs.

188. Make sure donors or members know where their money is going.

Your gift of x dollars pays for y. Your dues pay for z through zz.

189. Conduct a raffle.

It's old school, inexpensive, and a crowd pleaser, but that doesn't mean the prize can be just anything. It has to be something people want, whether it's the newest i-gadget or a couple of plane tickets.

190. Hire an artist to complete a painting onsite at your next big event, and then auction it off as a fundraiser or to benefit a charity at the end of the event.

Be sure to promote the idea ahead of time so people know what to expect.

191. Format a fundraising appeal like a Dutch auction.

Send out a series of emails asking for decreasing donation amounts, and at each stage eliminate those who give from the email list.

192. Make it mobile.

Conduct a fundraising campaign that collects donations via text messages. In a text-donation campaign, a supporter can text a special code to a specified number in order to have a donation added to his or her monthly mobile phone bill. The mobile service provider sends the donated amount to the organization.

193. Put your volunteers to work asking for money.

It doesn't have to be small change. If you think they have the potential to bring in the big bucks that come with corporate sponsorship, invest in training them, developing talking points, providing them with materials. Or better yet, find a volunteer with expertise to do it for you.

8 Ways to Increase Member Involvement in Fundraising

1. Use those who have benefited from a fundraising effort as real voices in your campaign. For example, tap into those who have received scholarships or recognitions that were key to their career development.

2. Make members the "building blocks" for a fundraising effort. For example, publicize the names of members who have contributed (gifts large and small) as giving not just dollars but contributing to the success of the fundraising effort.

3. Link fundraising campaigns with important association accomplishments—for example, ask people to donate $70 for the 70th anniversary, associate a campaign with the association's founding members, and so forth.

4. Members will identify with a fundraising effort that also speaks to their personal contribution to the legacy of the organization. If a gift, great or small, builds or expands upon the profession and its mission, then a member will want to be a part of contributing to the legacy.

5. Offer members opportunities to leverage small gifts through challenge grants and matching gift programs. These incentives can also be used to encourage first-time members.

6. Clearly communicate to members an association's need for funds. The appeal should be purpose-driven. Then, engage the membership in realizing not just the financial goal but the fulfillment of an organizational need.

7. Demonstrate accountability and build visibility for a giving program by reporting publicly about its results and its impact on the mission.

8. Celebrate a success directly with members—have a party! Nothing succeeds like success.

Reprinted from *The Decision to Give: What Motivates Individuals to Support Professional Associations*, 2010 ASAE & The Center for Association Leadership

MISCELLANY

194. Bring together your chapters to share information about revenue sources.
What works for one may work for others or could be the seed for a new national program.

195. If you've identified potential new markets outside of your membership, but don't know how to reach them, look for a partner who can.
Partners who are interested in promoting and selling your existing products or services to their members may also be interested in working together to develop new offerings that will benefit both their members and yours.

196. Take advantage of opportunities to collaborate.
If you have a chance to get together with representatives of similar organizations, do it. You might learn something or make a connection that saves you the time and expense of recreating the wheel.

197. Rent your list…or not.
You may have been renting out your members' mailing addresses for years, but do you balk at renting out their email addresses? You can generate nondues revenue and protect your members at the same time by offering vendors an alternative. Rather than rent out the e-list, sell vendors the opportunity to send a message through you. You'll be doing your members a favor by controlling access to their

in-boxes and helping manage the number and content of messages they do receive.

198. If you sell merchandise, promote the lower-cost items with highest margins.

These might include wristbands, t-shirts, reusable grocery bags, car magnets, or decals, etc. Use these as add-ons or impulse orders at check-out to increase your overall margin per order. Also, don't just use a flat percentage for margin. Check out competition and retail outlets for pricing guidance.

199. Update your look.

If you have an existing credential program and have lapel pins or certificates, you can update the design and sell the new ones through your storefront. Newer styles of pins and certificate holders will be often more attractive and will sell to those who want to show they're au currant. Pins or certificate holders can be purchased wholesale and sold at retail prices. Display samples at all events. Changing your association's logo may also generate revenue by driving sales of new logo merchandise.

BIBLIOGRAPHY

Associapedia entry: Hosted Buyer Tradeshow.

Athitakis, Mark. "Keeping Membership Strong in a Recession." *Associations Now*, June 2009.

Boucher, Michelle. "Partner Corner: Conference Technology." *Associations Now*, December 2009.

"Bring New Life to an Old Event." *Associations Now*, July 2010.

Bronislaw, Prokuski. "Anatomy of a Merger." *Association Management*, February 2002.

"CEO to CEO: Board Value; Cost-Cutting." *Associations Now*, September 2008.

"CEO to CEO: Pros and Cons of Yearly Versus Rolling Membership Cycles." *Association Management*, June 2005.

Chandler, Linda C. "Taking a Strategic Approach to Convention Publications." *Associations Now*, February 2006.

Clarke, Kristin. "Green Goals Save Money, Inspire Staff." *Associations Now*, November 2009.

Constantine, George E. and Jeffrey S. Tenenbaum. "IRS Issues: Virtual Trade Show Guidance." *Executive Update*, April 2005.

DiVincenzo, Robert S. "Getting International Donors Through Direct Mail." *Associations Now*, September 2008.

Dreyer, Lindy, Sarah Sears, and Steve Drake. "Social Media and Money: A Pre-Annual Meeting Chat." *Associations Now*, May 2010.

Dreyer, Lindy. "Talking About the Word-of-Mouth Revolution." *Associations Now*, January 2009.

Dunne, Joanne E. "Financial Efficiency for Associations." *Associations Now*, May 2009.

Dysart, Joe. "Sold: A One-time Skeptic's Guide to Online Auctions." *Executive Update*, April 2004.

Farnham, Peter. "Cashing in on Internet Job Banks." *Executive Update*, May 2003.

Faust, Summer. "6 Steps to Recruitment Success." *Associations Now*, September 2009.

Fernandez, Kim. "Choose Your Nondues Revenue." *Associations Now*, May 2009.

Fernandez, Kim. "Finding Space for Success." *Associations Now*, February 2009.

Fernandez, Kim. "Is Your Lease Negotiable?" *Associations Now*, August 2009.

Fernandez, Kim. "Stand Out in the Crowd: Marketing at the Annual Meeting." *Associations Now*, January 2009.

"Fundraisers Expect Difficult Times." *Associations Now*, May 2009.

Gardner, Michael. "Protecting Your Organization's Assets." *Associations Now*, January 2009.

"Going Once, Going Twice…Your Advertising Is Sold!" *Associations Now*, September 2009.

Heinan, Landa. "Planning Predictable IT Budgets." *Associations Now*, December 2007.

"Helping Members in Hard Times." *Associations Now*, January 2009.

Hill, Ruth A. "How a DMC Can Help." *Associations Now*, December 2009.

"Idea Bank: Turn Your Next Event into a Work of Art." *Associations Now*, July 2008.

Jackson, Nancy Mann. "Trade Up Your Tradeshow Model." *Associations Now*, May 2010.

Karen, Jay. "Lessons From Failure: Growing Affinity." *Associations Now*, September 2008.

Kelly, Douglas R. "Advertising 2.0." *Associations Now*, March 2010.

Kerr, Harold. "Guide to Tech Solutions: The Home-Grown Social Media Platform." *Associations Now*, June 2009.

Kiernan, Kathy. "Partner Corner: Managing Energy Costs and Efficiencies." *Associations Now*, May 2010.

"Knowledge Center FAQs: Ad Sales." *Associations Now*, December 2009.

"Knowledge Center FAQs: Explaining Dues Increases." *Associations Now,*
March 2010.

Krughoff, Tracy. "Listen to Members for Meeting Success." *Associations Now,*
January 2010.

Lang, Andrew. "Cost Controls Boost the Bottom Line." *Associations Now,* July
2010.

Lang, Andrew. "New Markets, New Revenue." *Associations Now,* November
2009.

Lang, Andrew. "New Money: Distribution Overhaul." *Associations Now,*
September 2009.

Lang, Andrew. "Outsmarting the Economy." *Executive Update,* January 2002.

Lang, Andrew. "Revitalizing Existing Revenue Streams." *Associations Now,*
June 2010.

Lang, Andrew. "Right Thinking Leads to New Revenue." *Associations Now,*
December 2009.

Lang, Andrew. "When the Price Isn't Right." *Associations Now,* September
2008.

Leigh, Edward. "Cultivating Corporate Relationships." *Association
Management,* September 2004.

Magnuson, Peter J. "Clean Slate: Making a Good Publication Better."
Executive Update, November 2003.

Mead, Chris. "Finding Money in New Places." *Executive Update,* February
2004.

Morgan, Jeffrey D. "Disaster Doctrine." *Association Management,* September
2003.

Motley, Apryl. "Growing Nondues Revenue." *Association Management,* August
2005.

Motley, Apryl. "In the Move Groove." *Associations Now,* October 2005.

Newman, Diana S. "$ense and $ensitivity: Keys to Attracting Diverse
Donors." *Executive Update,* August 2003.

"News & Know-How: Preventing or Minimizing Attrition." *Association
Management,* November 2004.

"Operator, Will You Help Me Place This Call?" *Associations Now,* April 2009.

Pelletier, Stephen. "Investment Strategies for Volatile Markets." *Associations
Now,* March 2009.

"Picture This: Free Photography for Your Publication." *Associations Now*, May 2010.

Pina, Mike. "Capitalize on Your Pressroom." *Association Management*, August 2005.

Powell, Thomas. "Getting the Word Out." *Association Management*, September 2005.

Rominiecki, Joe. "Make the Move to Mobile." *Associations Now*, August 2009.

Rossell, Toni. "7 Proven Ways to Grow Your Membership." *Associations Now*, July 2010.

Sabo, Sandra. "Wrapping It Up." *Association Management*, March 2002.

Schweitzer, Carole. "A Different Breed of Budgeting." *Association Management*, January 2003.

Skillman, Keith C. "Successful Telecommuting." *Associations Now*, September 2008.

Steggles, Andy. "Serve Your Mission With Mobile Technology." *Associations Now*, July 2010.

Tenenbaum, Jeffrey S. "Legal and Tax Considerations for Capital Campaigns." *Center Collection Model*, May 2002.

Truesdell, Mark. "Conducting a Raffle." *Association Management*, September 2005.

Uppercue, Crystal. "Power Up Your Marketing Toolbelt." *Associations Now*, June 2008.

Waddle, Jeff. "Don't Let Currency Changes Break the Bank." *Associations Now*, June 2008.

Waddle, Jeff. "Protect Your Association From Room-Block 'Pirates.'" *Associations Now*, March 2009.

White, Aria. "Two Associations, One Office." *Associations Now*, January 2010.

Whitehorne, Samantha. "Favorable Forecast." *Associations Now*, May 2007.

Williams, Monica. "The Care and Feeding of Your Renewal Strategy." *Association Management*, June 2003.

Worth, Steven. "International Growth: A Look at Four Options." *Executive Update*, September 2003.

SHARE TIPS WITH COLLEAGUES

In our ongoing effort to connect great ideas and great people, we're collecting tips and ideas on a variety of topics that will be reviewed, and *if selected,* will be published in a future publication—a collection of "199" tips on a particular topic. You can choose to be credited as a contributor and if your tip is published be listed in the book as such, or you can choose to remain anonymous. Either way, it's a chance to give back to your profession and help others achieve greater success.

If you have questions about our "199 Ideas" series, please contact the director of book publishing at books@asaecenter.org.

Following is the submission form. We prefer that you visit www.asaecenter.org/sharemytip to submit your tip electronically via our website. However, if you prefer, you may copy and submit the form by mail or fax to:

Attn: Director of Book Publishing
ASAE: The Center for Association Leadership
1575 I Street, NW
Washington, DC 20005-1103
Fax: (202) 220-6439

Share My Tip Form

Please select the appropriate category or categories for your tip submission:

Board & Volunteers
- ☐ Board Relations
- ☐ Volunteer Relations
- ☐ Volunteer Recruitment
- ☐ Volunteer Engagement
- ☐ Volunteer Retention/Rewarding

Meetings
- ☐ Sponsorships
- ☐ Connecting Attendees
- ☐ Exhibits
- ☐ Generating Additional Revenue
- ☐ Other: _____

Finance
- ☐ Budgeting
- ☐ Cutting Expenses
- ☐ Other: _____

Benchmarking & Research
- ☐ Increasing Response Rate
- ☐ Other: _____

Membership
- ☐ Recruitment/Retention
- ☐ Communications
- ☐ Engagement
- ☐ Program Benefits
- ☐ Dues Structures
- ☐ Globalization
- ☐ Research
- ☐ Other: _____

Technology
- ☐ Other: _____

Time-Saving Tips
- ☐ Other: _____

Please submit your tip below. Please limit to 500 characters. If you require more than 500 characters, please submit via email directly to books@asaecenter.org with the subject "Tip".

_____

_____

_____

_____

_____

_____

_____

_____

_____

_____

_____

_____

Continued on next page

Share My Tip Form
continued from previous page

Name: _____

Organization: _____

_____

Email: _____

Please indicate whether you would like to remain anonymous or be credited as a tip contributor if your tip is published:

☐ Anonymous

☐ Yes, please list me as a contributor.

By submitting your tip, you represent and warrant that you are the sole author and proprietor of all rights in the work, that the work is original, that the work has not been previously published, that the work does not infringe any personal or property rights of another, that the work does not contain anything libelous or otherwise illegal, and that you have the authority to enter into this agreement and grant of license. You also agree that the work contains no material from other works protected by copyright that have been used without the written consent of the copyright owner and that ASAE: The Center for Association Leadership is under no obligation to publish your tip submission.

You also grant ASAE: The Center for Association Leadership the following rights: (1) to publish the work in all print, digital, and other known or unknown formats; (2) to reprint, make derivative works of, and otherwise reproduce the work in all print, digital, and other known or unknown formats; and (3) to grant limited sub-licenses to others for the right to reprint, make derivative works of, and otherwise reproduce the work in all print, digital, and other known or unknown formats.

Signature _____

k you for submitting your tip!

Share My Tip Form

Please select the appropriate category or categories for your tip submission:

Board & Volunteers
- ☐ Board Relations
- ☐ Volunteer Relations
- ☐ Volunteer Recruitment
- ☐ Volunteer Engagement
- ☐ Volunteer Retention/Rewarding

Meetings
- ☐ Sponsorships
- ☐ Connecting Attendees
- ☐ Exhibits
- ☐ Generating Additional Revenue
- ☐ Other: _____

Finance
- ☐ Budgeting
- ☐ Cutting Expenses
- ☐ Other: _____

Benchmarking & Research
- ☐ Increasing Response Rate
- ☐ Other: _____

Membership
- ☐ Recruitment/Retention
- ☐ Communications
- ☐ Engagement
- ☐ Program Benefits
- ☐ Dues Structures
- ☐ Globalization
- ☐ Research
- ☐ Other: _____

Technology
- ☐ Other: _____

Time-Saving Tips
- ☐ Other: _____

Please submit your tip below. Please limit to 500 characters. If you require more than 500 characters, please submit via email directly to books@asaecenter.org with the subject "Tip".

_____
_____
_____
_____
_____
_____
_____
_____
_____
_____
_____

Continued on next page...

Share My Tip Form

continued from previous page

Name: ....

Organization: ....

....

Email: ....

Please indicate whether you would like to remain anonymous or be credited as a tip contributor if your tip is published:

☐ Anonymous

☐ Yes, please list me as a contributor.

By submitting your tip, you represent and warrant that you are the sole author and proprietor of all rights in the work, that the work is original, that the work has not been previously published, that the work does not infringe any personal or property rights of another, that the work does not contain anything libelous or otherwise illegal, and that you have the authority to enter into this agreement and grant of license. You also agree that the work contains no material from other works protected by copyright that have been used without the written consent of the copyright owner and that ASAE: The Center for Association Leadership is under no obligation to publish your tip submission.

You also grant ASAE: The Center for Association Leadership the following rights: (1) to publish the work in all print, digital, and other known or unknown formats; (2) to reprint, make derivative works of, and otherwise reproduce the work in all print, digital, and other known or unknown formats; and (3) to grant limited sub-licenses to others for the right to reprint, make derivative works of, and otherwise reproduce the work in all print, digital, and other known or unknown formats.

Signature ....

Thank you for submitting your tip!